THE A to Z
OF EFFECTIVE
COMMUNICATION
A POCKET PRIMER

First published in 2020
AUTHOR Wendy Smith
DESIGNER Caroline Jefford
ILLUSTRATIONS Simonetta d'Ottaviano
CREATIVE DIRECTION Raymonde Watkins

WHO IS THIS BOOK FOR?

Quite simply anyone who wants to get the most out of everyday communication through to the pitch of their life.

Fine tuning our communication skills can help in so many ways, from the visible – winning that pitch with the perfect piece of persuasion – to the invisible, such as acts of situation reading that can help to avoid conflict and spread a little joy.

Whether you are a teacher in a school, a student in a classroom, or an office worker, getting your point across counts to both you and the recipient.

This book has been constructed to give you 26 hints and tips to make your social and business interactions that much more effective.

ENJOY!

INTRODUCTION

Communicating: it's easy stuff; you just open your mouth and talk, don't you? Well, perhaps not. We have all had those moments when we have got it oh so wrong. The tongue has engaged well before the brain, and out of your mouth has come that big, disastrous statement. The message has crash-landed, and that gaffe has cost you the friend, the job, the relationship...

As we become more and more information rich and time poor, being concise and communicating appropriately is becoming more important than ever. Whatever stage in life we are at – whether we're going through school, university, the working world or socialising generally – we all need to communicate. It doesn't matter whether we are simply shooting the breeze with friends and family or giving a high-powered presentation to the chairman of the board; being effective matters.

So, what do we mean by effective? Simply, it means just being understood – and there are solutions that can help you along the tricky path of getting what you really mean to say heard by those who really need to listen.

This is where this handy guide to the essentials of communication comes in. In this book, you will find tips to help you along the way, including checks to put into place when talking, pitching, presenting... this A to Z contains basic tips and pointers for you to read and instantly apply in your everyday life.

No-one is a natural communicator, and the best out there have worked hard – very hard – to perfect their skills. So, what does it take to be the best? You need the ability to listen and observe others, and, dare we say it, a passion for your subject. As with everything, it is all the small steps (using the right word, having the correct posture or honing your message) that will make all the difference to achieving better outcomes. It will not come overnight, but you really will develop your skills as a communicator.

Good luck!

Audience

Analysing your audience is a good place to start. The first rule here is that your audience is important – MUCH more important than you.

Think of your message as a game of catch and your audience as the other players. Simple playground stuff. A throws to B, and B catches the ball – (well, hopefully). If you don't know how quick they are to the ball, what their hand–eye coordination is like, how tall or short they are or, how far away from you they are, and you indiscriminately lob your tennis balls at them and miss – disaster. If this ball is your message, how many of your audience members will stand a chance of getting it? Not many. And how fed up will they be to be left out of the game?

Do this at your peril. They – the members of your audience – are the important ones, not you. They will not take kindly to you (or whomever you are representing). Even the greatest performers can get booed off stage if they are late or sing songs that people don't want to hear. Do your homework first.

> **Hints and tips**
> Arrive early to introduce yourself to people and get a feel for the mood. This will help you to connect accordingly, gauge the mood and retune your energy levels appropriately.

Breathing

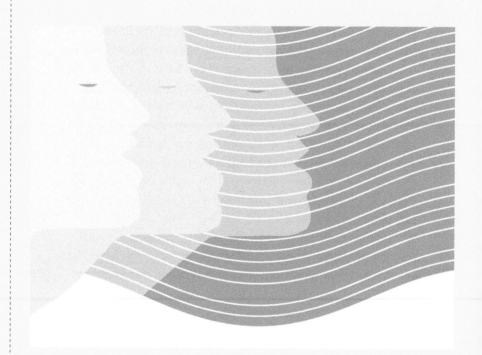

There is one main reason why we all breathe – to carry on living.
Correct breathing is also vital for performance. There are different
ways of breathing – from the nervous, short, shallow breaths that we
take when we are in fight-or-flight mode to the deep, calming breaths
of someone prepared, confident and in control.

As any singer will tell you, natural diaphragmatic breathing
takes years of training but is vital to their trade. A useful tip is to
check the tension in your body. Where are your shoulders? Are they
tense and shooting up towards your ears? If so, relax them down
and let them flop downwards.

Replying on short pants of breath will restrict oxygen intake
to the brain and make a speaker lightheaded. It will also prevent

them from thinking clearly.
Not doing so will lead to
confusion, poor memory
and a lack of confidence.

Breathe slowly and
inhale down to your lower
abdomen. Put your hand
on your stomach and feel it
move up and down. Breathe
in and hold, and then

breathe out slowly to a count of ten. Get oxygen into your body and
allow your brain to work. Great presenters and performers will always
prepare, and a really useful way is quite simply to sing. Singing will
warm up your vocal cords and possibly make you laugh, which will
produce those really helpful feel-good endorphins.

Credibility

Credibility is the core of your presence, and the key to credibility is knowledge. Simply put, demonstrating appropriate knowledge and transferring it properly can be described as delivering 'the right message, at the right time, to the right people'.

You may well be an expert in your subject, but you still need to demonstrate this to your audience. Very few of them will bother to research you before they meet you.

Questions to consider: Are you informing people about your professional background and experience – and therefore giving your audience confidence in you and making the audience aware of your professional gravitas? Are you putting the subject you are talking about in context? Are you describing the challenges that you/the market/your research is facing?

Credibility also means looking the part. Mirror your audience at least, or even go slightly smarter. Clothes do matter. Shirts need to be ironed and footwear must be clean. Jewellery should be appropriate and complementary to your style rather than distracting or overwhelming.

> Hints and tips
>
> If you are meeting people in a networking context, make sure to position yourself professionally with a well-structured elevator pitch. However, this will need fine–tuning and adapting according to different scenarios.

Delivery

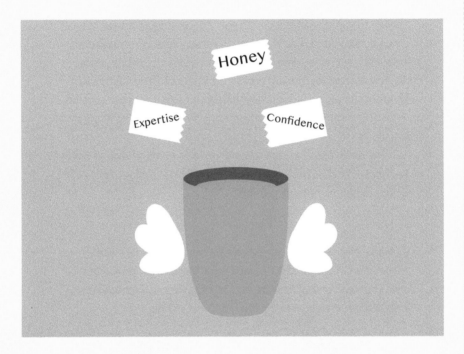

All the prep and the most fabulous slide deck in the world will not protect you if you mess up your actual delivery. The most fundamental point to bear in mind is that your audience wants you to be good. If you are not passionate about what you have to say, then who will be?

To ensure you get the words out, get your head into gear. Confidence is in the mind. Do not allow those evil gremlins to get inside your psyche and tell you right at the last minute what you can't do; instead, visualise the angel on your shoulder to tell you what you can. Remind yourself of your successes and how you have earned the right to be asked to stand in front of this audience. You are an expert in this subject, you have worked hard to craft the right message, so you owe it to your audience to deliver it to the best of your ability.

Now that you've finished with your head, what about your voice? It is well documented that Margaret Thatcher softened her voice with warm water and honey, and Tony Blair always warmed up his vocal cords before speaking. Record yourself to check out any quirks you may not have noticed before. Play with your voice. Take your tone up and down occasionally to avoid monotony. Practise smiling at your audience.

Some quick tips: hum to loosen your vocal cords, and drink water to wet your throat. If you can, stretch and run on the spot to get air into your lungs and remove tension.

> ### Hints and tips
> Smiling when you talk really does make your voice sound both warmer and friendlier. This is because the vocal cords are pulled differently than when you aren't smiling. Also, the very act of smiling will help both you and your listeners relax into the message or conversation.

Empathy

Empathy means getting on the same wavelength as your audience. It means getting inside the heads of the people you will be presenting to and finding the right messages that will connect with what they want to hear. What do you know about the members of your audience? Are they all senior-level people? Is the organisation going through a restructure? Have there recently been changes at the top? What are their ages and backgrounds?

Each group creates its own specific mood, and you need to be able to sense this. Get in the room and, if you have time, introduce yourself to a few people. Check out the person sitting at the back with their arms folded across their chest. Acknowledge their presence. They may have a fixed furrow on their brow and be exuding a bad temper, but this is probably nothing to do with you. You can help the dynamics along by at least making eye contact and smiling. Making them feel included can go some way to improving the atmosphere in the room. Once you have done this you can adjust your tone and language accordingly to get the best results for everyone.

Hints and tips

Check out the names of the delegates in the room to give you some kind of steer as to the age range of the people in front of you. Your Susans will probably be Baby Boomers, alongside the Jeremys and Christines. The Jacobs, Joshuas and Matts are more likely to be Millennials or Gen Zers.

Fillers

So, what is filler? Well, um, err, like, you know, what, I mean, so…
We all have our little vocal ticks. The words we all fall back on for
comfort when we are searching for the next thing to come out of
our mouths. They may be comforting for us, but they can be really
annoying for those who have to listen to them. If you are studying
English as a foreign language, you may be encouraged to learn the
fillers for fluency, and of course they have their place in general
conversation to soften a point or emphasise an issue.

However, when you are on a stage delivering a message,
overuse of fillers can suggest an attack of nerves, a lack
of preparation, or to some kinds of audience, a lack of respect.
The higher your filler count, the more you risk losing your audience.

Need some tips to eradicate fillers? First, ask yourself what
your favourite over-used words are. I had a friend who pointed out
how much I said 'excellent'. Since then, it's probably been replaced
with 'wow'. Record yourself, or ask your friends and family which
words you overuse. Listen to the ones they use and check whether
your over-use rate compares.

In public speaking, the cure for fillers is in the preparation.

Hints and tips

In the age of Zoom and teleconferences, where there may well be
people on a call presenting who you can't see, enter, stage left, the
pretty valuable discourse marker. As opposed to standard fillers,
discourse markers (oh, well, I see) are necessary to let the speaker
know you are engaged with what they are saying. These small vocal
utterances at the right moment with the appropriate tonality really do
help reassure the speaker (and any others who are listening) that you are
engaging too.

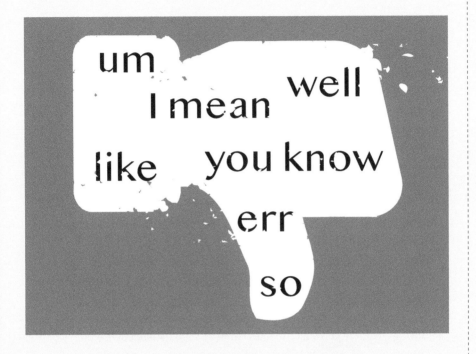

The more confident and rehearsed you are, the less likely you are to let your eyes wander while your brain churns round for the next point you want to make. Visualise that full stop at the end of the point you are making. It is there for a purpose. See that full stop in your mind, pause and breathe. There – the filler has gone.

Gestures

Did you know that, according to the communication model introduced by Albert Mehrabian in the 1970s, we only listen to seven per cent of the actual messages we hear? A long time ago humans didn't have the sophisticated speech and language we use today, so they were dependent on grunts, groans and non-verbal communications – gestures, facial expressions, posture. Mehrabian says that the use of our voice (tone, intonation and volume) influences only 38 per cent of our message; the rest is determined by – yes, you've got it – our body language.

Our non-verbal gestures really show what we are feeling, and they need to be in tune with what we are actually saying; to be convincing, our gestures and spoken words need to support each other. It's like when you walk into a store for service and the sales assistant is smiling with their mouth, but their eyes are telling a different story. That smile becomes a grimace.

So, to remind ourselves, body language is generally a bit like driving a car. We know all the rules – mirror, signal, manoeuvre – but sometimes, we get a bit sloppy. With communication, we need to remind ourselves to check that our physical gestures are as one with the message we are putting across. If, for example, you are trying to convince someone, it is better to engage by leaning in towards them rather than slouching back in your chair. The important thing is to support the message rather than detracting from it.

> **Hints and tips**
>
> The gesture game changes slightly in the area of communicating via a screen. Your frame is limited – big, wide gestures will not be a great tactic to pull your audience in metaphorically to embrace your message. The small screen requires different body language checks. David Straun, vocal coach and actor, advises keeping gestures deliberate and small in video conferencing.

Humour

The 'H-word' can be dangerous stuff. Many of us have experienced telling a 'funny' story that people simply don't find funny at all. There are presenters out there who are simply brilliant at this kind of stuff, but that group possibly does not include you. The phrase 'I have to share a funny story with you' can have an audience thinking, 'Oh no, you don't!'.

Avoid jokes, as the risk is too high. I have sat through offensive sexist jokes and horrendous Irish jokes and wanted to crawl under my table. However, a good-natured story delivered well with witty asides is great if you can carry it off with confidence. It can really lift an audience. Self-deprecating humour works best, but go easy on that as overdoing it can inadvertently undermine your gravitas. Remember: you are pitching yourself as an acknowledged expert, so avoid undermining yourself.

However, when used confidently and appropriately, humour has many benefits. Remember to check out the demographics of the room to make sure your listeners are culturally receptive and in the right age range to 'get' your humour. And, if they do laugh, let it roll until they've finished. If they don't, just smile and keep on going.

A well-positioned and well-intentioned bit of humour can be magical when it relaxes the audience, enforces a point and builds rapport. A good laugh can subtly shift the 'you up there on the stage' aspect of a presentation to a far more collegial, 'we are all sharing a joke here' mood.

> **Hints and tips**
> Always try to be self-deprecating – why not recall a personal story and share with your listeners what you learned? A win–win situation here. They laugh and relax, and everyone learns something.

Information

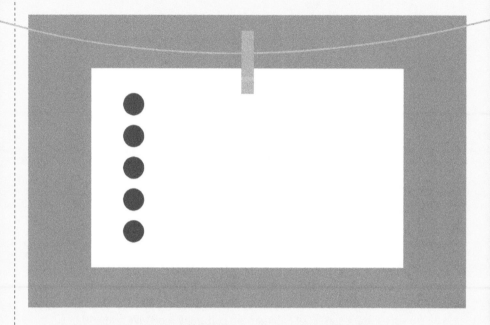

One of the most valuable things I learned from hearing the linguist David Crystal speak in London was never to drop in a vital piece of information or key message right at the beginning of your talk. Why? Your listeners are too busy working out their place in the room, their comfort level and the acoustics to take in anything big at the start. This, Crystal explained, is the light, introductory moment. Give them at least five minutes, and then serve up the big stuff.

The good thing about information is that, when presenting, you are invariably the subject expert. The reason why you have been asked to deliver is that you do have the information that people want, and now it's down to you to deliver it in a way they can understand.

Remember: we all have our preferred ways of learning and

taking in information. For many, hearing is enough; others like a more show-and-tell approach. If you are presenting a project with a fixed product at the end, make sure to show it to your audience.

I like hearing about hard facts and/or statistics in a way I can access. If it is a statistic to underpin the veracity of a statement, give me a visual I can see – I love a pie chart or a histogram. If you are putting information into your PowerPoint, make sure that you pre-test it to ensure that the audience members at the back of the room can actually see it without having to squint.

Information doesn't always have to be a hard fact – it can simply be a picture. A single image is often hugely powerful. Watch how the best presenters and communicators keep their slides pure and powerful.

A word about clutter. Time and time again, people get over-excited about the amount of information that is presented on one slide. Your audience can't take it in. Keep to no more than five bullet points per slide.

Jargon

Jargon is defined as the use of specific phrases and words in a particular situation, profession or trade. These specialised terms are used to convey meanings that are accepted and understood in that field.

If you are sure your audience is made up purely of people from your own specific industry, then, of course, jargon is acceptable and probably expected – to a certain extent. It is your professional shorthand. However, beware of using it for the sake of it or deluding yourself that it makes you sound clever. It could have the negative effect of simply making you sound arrogant and excluding the very people you wish to communicate with.

Listen to business meetings and jot down the number of times 'faddish' language is used. Where did the overuse of 'going forward' come from? Expressions go in and out of fashion precisely because they add nothing to the communication process. A particularly irritating one was 'suck it and see!'

Acronyms may be highly useful written down (although – always remember to write out the term in full first), they can lose an audience as soon as uttered out loud. People may either not hear the acronym properly or not know it. Either way, you may lose them while they check with a colleague next to them what you're on about.

> **Hints and tips**
> Use jargon wisely when you communicate, and help people out by demystifying any terms that may be unclear. When in doubt, leave it out.

Key messages

Whenever we communicate, we do so for a reason – to get a specific message across to the person or people listening. We want an outcome. We want the listener to clearly understand our messages and make a different choice of direction.

But are they in the right mood to receive our message? All good salespeople know that they have to achieve that emotional buy-in before commitment. The speaker has to care so that the listener(s) will care.

However, issues often arises when we make the mistake of attempting to hit our audience over the head with too much information in a wave of unbridled enthusiasm. They can end up mired in detail and not hear a thing.

This is where we have to ensure that the key messages we

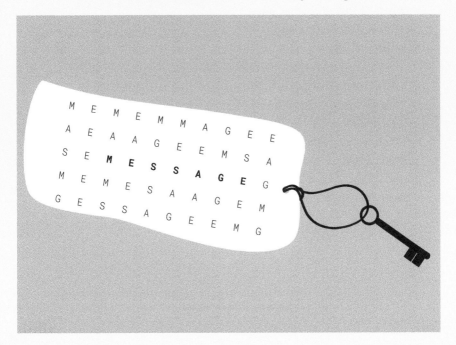

choose are crafted and linked appropriately.

What we are doing here is signposting our audience. We should begin with who we are and the reason why we're there. We then manage their expectations about how long we will take and then we move swiftly on to what we will talk about and the why. Some people call this the situation (context): what is happening now, why it should change, the recommended solution, and how that will happen.

Hints and tips

Voice coach and actress Kate Terris demonstrates this technique to great effect: if you want to ensure your key message is simple and understandable, try it out on the youngest member of your family. Get down to their level and really learn about the clarity and brevity you need to boil down what you're saying. This can be humbling, and even humiliating for some, but it works at treat every time.

A good presenter/communicator should be able to achieve this in a 30-second elevator pitch. Test yourself on this. The stumbling block is always the why. Why in heaven's name is your input going to make a difference? If you don't know, chances are that it will be game over with your audience. A simple formula is to set out your structure: who you are, what you are doing, why you are doing it, and then how you will do it. If you talk about the how at the beginning, you will have a confused audience at the end.

Listening

Listening properly, or active listening, is really hard work. It means making a real concerted effort to hear something – truly paying attention to what is being said, how it is being said and the sound of it. It is a part of being actively involved in the conversation, and it gives the speaker the confidence that they are being heard and understood.

The key thing that we all need to hardwire into our heads is that we should be listening to understand, rather than listening simply to hear. How many times have you witnessed people in a conversation, where one person barely finishes off their sentence before the other hijacks the subject and switches it back to themselves?

Empathic listening takes time, but it doesn't take anywhere nearly as much time as it takes to back up and correct misunderstandings further down the line. Retrospective repeating and explaining can so often leave the speaker thinking, 'if only I had listened properly!'.

Active listeners ask questions in meetings and forums – both open and closed. They then go on to verify their understanding: – 'so what you want is', 'what I understand your need to be is…'.

Curb the tendency to jump in. We are all guilty of this one, especially if we're impatient or think we know the answers or feel we're on a tight schedule. Listen to what the speaker is actually saying and pitch your reply accordingly.

Hints and tips

When an audience member speaks up, paraphrase back to them what you have heard. Demonstrate that you have grasped the real intentions behind their comments. Take this opportunity to really show that, not only have you listened, but you really care about what is being asked or said. This will build empathy and trust with your audience.

Memory

Memory is hugely relevant to both you as the communicator and those with whom you are communicating. Supremely confident presenters can deliver their talks totally from memory, simply using PowerPoint slides as visual prompts. Some people rely on the failsafe of cards with points to prompt them, while others write out the whole presentation.

Whichever method you choose, practise, practise and practise again. I have worked with designers presenting for 30 minutes who put in 12 hours of prep. I have delivered a three-minute speech that took several hours to fine tune. You cannot rely on thinking it over in the back of taxi on the way to the meeting. Your audience will be able to tell if you haven't done your homework, and they will feel

disrespected that you have not given them the courtesy of a decently thought-out delivery. Of course, nerves will play havoc with your brain as the memory mist descends, but with preparation, practise and correct breathing, much of this can be allayed.

Then there is the question of what your audience will remember from your talk. Keep your words simple and to the point.

Whatever language you are speaking, 'the rule of three' is still one of the oldest tricks out there. There are three 'tell'ums': you tell them at the beginning, you tell them in the middle again and you conclude with your last tell'um. This technique is all about reinforcement of learning in the memory.

Narrative

How we all love a story. It's the personal bit about how you came to be involved, why you are making your big statement, what you bring to the party and what past experiences you have to back it all up. Remember that a personal narrative can help a lot in presentations.

I once witnessed a hugely charming entrepreneur launching a new range of drinks. His products were exquisite, and his general delivery was fine. But the feedback from the audience was interesting – they wanted hear more about his own story and the inspiration behind his fabulous ideas.

It might sound a bit cheesy, but a well-rehearsed segment on your personal background with a great punchline will work every time. So, tell your story, but don't get too tearful in the telling. Passion and enthusiasm are one thing, but real tears can be very uncomfortable for an audience. Tears tell the story that this is about you and not about them. If you feel that the subject is too revealing and pressing a button you can't control , it's best to leave it out.

Working with your own personal emotions can be tough. Try, rehearsing in front of a trusted friend, colleague or family member. Go through the delivery, reading it as many times as possible. Remove any words that are too uncomfortable for you to say, and replace them if necessary. Make sure you get the pace right and that all the words are appropriate. In constructing your narrative, it is important to avoid material that is mawkish or voyeuristic.

> Hints and tips
>
> Make sure that the story you are about to tell your audience has a point that is relevant to them. And make sure you tell them at the beginning. Don't try and let them work it out themselves, or things might get too confusing and destroy the flow of your talk.

Overconfidence

Entitled, cocky presenters are the people who won't listen when told that they need to put the work in beforehand – they won't prepare or practise to ensure they deliver their best performance. These people are members of a club labelled 'prepare on the way to the event', 'write it on the back of an envelope' or 'done it all before'.

However, no two events and no two audiences are ever the same. Moods shift and atmospheres change like time and the weather. In this context, nerves really do help. Nerves produce the flow of adrenaline we all need to give us that sharpness – that edge – that we need to convey to our audience. Nerves tell the audience you care about them and really want to do well. Take that away, and your audience will notice.

Overconfidence will scream out of your body language, ooze out of the tonality in your voice and exude a lack of concern. Two things may happen here. You might wake up in the middle of your talk, realise that you really aren't connecting and raise your game, or the audience will exact their revenge. Just watch those nasty questions fly at the end.

Overconfidence is quite simply an excessive belief in one's own abilities. Any whiff of arrogance gets picked up and can be deeply unpleasant and off-putting to witness. It's a real turn-off.

> **Hints and tips**
>
> That need to over-egg your self-importance can simply reflect a lack of confidence. Deep down, an overly confident person is actually under-confident. How to solve this? Really know your subject, practise and get feedback.

Pause

The power of the pause is well known in any kind of communication. You pause to show that you have taken in a piece of information. You pause to give the listener time to digest what you have said before moving on. You pause to breathe. Then, there is the dramatic effect of the pause. This is where your silence gets your audience to sit up and take notice – particularly if you hold their collective gaze at the same time.

'P' also stands for posture. This is one of the first things anyone with performance training will talk about when presenting. The word they will use is 'grounded'. How you show yourself physically is how you show yourself mentally. You may want to use the space by walking around to make contact with different parts of the

audience and create interest (although beware of making this look like a frenetic pacing exercise). You may prefer to stay at a central point.

Whatever you choose, start off with your feet shoulder-width apart and pointing towards your audience. Check that your shoulders are down and not scrunched up towards your ears. Image a piece of string being pulled from the top of your head towards the ceiling and breathe from your tummy, not from your upper chest. Get that air in. Walk tall and look them in the eye and this will kick-start your image as a confident, authoritative person who cares about their subject and their audience.

Pause and posture – a truly powerful cocktail to aid both drama and delivery.

Questions

The best tip here is to – prepare for the worst one ever. That dreaded query that you are not quite ready with an answer for. Of course, the best situation is when you really do have all the answers, but life isn't always like that. Never, ever lie – your body language will invariably give you away. If you don't know the answer, a gracious, 'thank you for asking that, it's a very important question' should be followed by an even more gracious, 'I will get back to you'.

In order to prepare for this situation, you and your team should add a question-and-answer session to your prep time. If you are in an interview situation, get a friend to go through scenarios with you beforehand and role play what might possibly come up.

When you are in the position of presenting, this is where you can dictate and take control over when and how you take questions. Most professionals will leave this until the end of, say, a 20-minute presentation, and then stipulate exactly how long they have to take queries from the audience. Remember to monitor the timing of this carefully and prompt with, 'we just have time for one more'.

Lying in wait in the audience is always the troublemaker – the person with that tell-tale whinge in their voice who was having a bad day even before they turned up at your talk. When they throw out an awkward or aggressive question, one tactic is to tell them you have noted their point and will deal with it afterwards. Another approach is to say you are short of time and need to get some more questions in. Always deliver this in a calm, measured manner. Never show your irritation as this is uncomfortable for the audience and weakens you.

> **Hints and tips**
>
> Just in case your audience is a bit apprehensive to kick-start a conversation with you, plant a question with a colleague to get the ball rolling or you can suggest a question yourself.

Relaxation

If you're too wired, you can't perform to the best of your ability.
If you're nervous and your mouth is dry, you're going to become
stressed. So, it is important to relax. Breathing techniques (see 'B')
can help in this context. You might also keep a bottle of water in
your hand and take a sip if you feel your mouth drying up. This also
serves as a chance for you and your audience to take a pause. Another
way to stop your mouth drying up is to bite the inside of your check
discreetly, which will release extra saliva.

If you are sweating, keep a hanky ready. Perhaps you could keep
a spare deodorant with you. And, if you feel sudden hunger pangs
and your stomach is churning, there's always the option of a banana.
Two strong cups of coffee can get some people in the zone, but it
may send others over the edge, making them start talking jibberish
at speed and sounding like a chipmunk. As for using alcohol to
relax before presenting, this a complete and utter no-no. A half-cut
presenter swaying at the lectern can be a gruesome spectacle.

> Hints and tips
> Before you start your talk, interview or video conference, and before the
> gremlins get into your head to puncture your confidence with negative
> thoughts, get your head in a happy space. Remind yourself of your most
> loved ones who think you are wonderful and positively reframe yourself
> and your achievements. A bit like the L'Oréal advert – you are there
> 'because you're worth it'.

Sound

Yes, I know. Nobody claims to like the sound of their own voice. Too shrill, too much of a regional accent, too flat... the list goes on. But remember that we always listen to ourselves through some kind of recording equipment, which distorts and alters our own sound. What really matters is that we know our voices and do our best work with them. Any singer will tell you that the sound that comes out of us is all about the breath we take in. So, visualise deep and low to get air into your belly. Practise breathing techniques to enrich the quality and duration of your vocal ability. And remember the calming benefits of a good, slow, breathe in and breathe out.

Having a regional accent doesn't matter – being understood does. The story has moved on from when you were frowned upon if you didn't sound like a 1950s BBC radio announcer. That clipped, received pronunciation is truly out of fashion. Regional is where it's at. Think about the Geordie accent and how it has entered the mainstream.

Trying to override your regional accent too much can sound false and be really off-putting. Just be yourself, articulate clearly and ensure you pronounce all the vowels and the ends of your words – don't swallow them. To modulate the sound of your voice, slow down!

The volume of the sound we make is another matter. If you are not sure how well the people at the back of the room will hear you, get a friend or colleague to stand at the back to test you for audibility. Also, remember that people themselves absorb sound: as the room fills up, you will need to crank up that extra bit of volume. But don't, in any circumstances, shout. Think of yourself breathing to the back of the room and carrying the volume with you.

Hints and tips

Take a moment and record your voice. Play it back. How does it sound? You may be pleasantly surprised. Play around with varying your speed, tone and pitch. And don't forget to smile to warm it all up.

Tone

Some of the world's best presenters have highlighted that it's all in the tonality. And they're right. Bear in mind that you need to vary your tone over the course of any talk. A flat, monotone delivery is what every audience dreads. I've sat through many presentations like this and just wished they would end. You don't want to be that person whose lack of tonality makes the presentation feel like it lasts forever. Again, get a trusted friend to listen to you to check for variation. Practise, play back and practise again to get your tone right.

Also, avoid the same repetition of tone (di-dum di-dum di-dum). This can have the same effect as the dreaded monotone – people just switch off and sleep through. You are not delivering bedtime poetry to children to get them to fall asleep. The key is variety and placing it where it will have maximum effect.

Hints and tips

Listen to people who deliver vocally with a variety of tones that you really like. Tune in to the professionals and see how they work their audience with tonal variations. Note the warmth in TV presenter Lorraine Kelly's voice presenting her morning breakfast show, or the firm-but-fair approach of Andrew Marr's delivery.

Up to date

Relevance really matters, so give your presentation that topical hook. Check that your information is up to date in the context of current world or local events. Monitor the news to see how events are unfolding and how you can link your information to current issues. If you are talking about a sustainable initiative, for example, you might link your message to current affairs in the wider green movement. What you are telling your audience also has to be relevant to what they want to hear. If you go off at a tangent, bring yourself back and check whether the point you are making is relevant to them. Avoid grandstanding on a current issue; your mantra should always be, 'what is in it for my audience?'

Perhaps you could check out research papers/reports for industry facts. Check out the news headlines in the week before your interview or presentation to make sure your material is on point and in tune with the latest thinking. Stepping out of your personal, philosophical or political silo is hugely valuable. You don't have to share or defend different views, but you do need to know they are out there. Being prepared and informed is the best position to be in.

Hints and tips

Check out with your colleagues in your field where they go for the most up-to-date, trustworthy and relevant information. Have a recording device on hand to capture the odd statistic or quote you think you may be able to use.

Variety

If you are delivering the same pitch or presentation or interview spiel time and time again, you will get bored. And guess what? When you're bored, so is your audience. To stay fresh, alert and enthusiastic, review your material and freshen it up – change the slides, introduce new ones, deliver another story, add a new case study – anything to keep you in the zone and your audience with you.

Hints and tips

When you change your slides for added variety and colour, make sure that your audience will still be able to see the information. Go to the back of the room and check. Is the typeface readable (always use a sans serif for clarity and legibility, especially for dyslexics in the room) and is the point size large enough?

Wrap

It's a wrap! You've reached the end. You may be glad that it's all over, but you don't need to share that with your audience. You need to 'land' your presentation with aplomb and care, not crash to the ground. Visualise your landing like a flight. We all appreciate the presenter who flags up the landing, summarises their key points, glides down to the ground and applies the brakes smoothly. Signal your availability after your talk with a simple, 'I'm happy to take questions now' or, 'I'll be available to chat over drinks'. Don't shudder to an abrupt halt, utter, 'that's me done' and shuffle off.

Endings are always tricky, but you should take heed from how the best journalists often literally wrap the story back to where they started with a reference to their entry point. This is always a neat trick. If you want to play it safe, then there is nothing wrong with thanking your audience for listening.

> **Hints and tips**
>
> Check out your speed of delivery with a colleague. Video yourself right to the end to double-check you finish at a steady, considered pace. Often, we are so keen to end our piece, we speed up from sheer nerves. This can kill any lasting impression you were hoping to make. And end with a smile if you can – it's that final facial footnote.

eXtra Mile

X – always a tricky one – is for the extra mile you must be prepared to go as a communicator if you want that new job, extra business or fresh investment. If you have worked hard, prepared properly, visualised your audience, practised your delivery, varied your tone, shown empathy and controlled your nerves effectively (all the things in this publication), your audience will know you have treated them with respect. Going the extra mile is the surest way to succeed. If you try to take shortcuts by just knocking it out the night before, your audience will rumble you.

> **Hints and tips**
>
> A thank-you email message after your talk or interview, or even a meet-up, will invariably impress the receiver – even if you don't get the pitch or the job. This may well put you in a better position to ask for some kind of feedback on why you didn't win this one!

You

I have put a lot of emphasis on the importance of the audience in this A–Z, but of course, it is also all about you. This is the bit about keeping it authentic. How people see you isn't about you putting on an unnatural accent that makes your face hurt or trying to be a Shakespearean actor – this is about you being yourself, with that extra bit of energy. Don't try to be who you're not, but do visualise what success would look like for you. Take a successful person into the room with you – yourself. As one of my formerly presentation-phobic clients said to me the other week, 'I actually found myself enjoying it!'.

You need to be physically fit as well as mentally fit before an important presentation. Much of this will rest in the preparation – and that extends to the night before. Keep your evening clear of any hectic social events, get a decent night's sleep, plan your journey to the venue, and anticipate the questions you may want to ask or may be asked. Putting work in equals getting results out.

> **Hints and tips**
>
> If you're taking a journey to a new venue, it is often the little things that can throw you. You may have covered off likely audience questions, dress code and your bottle of water, but what about the journey itself? Check it out. The things that tend to throw us are usually walking distance from a train station or the dreaded issue of parking.

Zoom

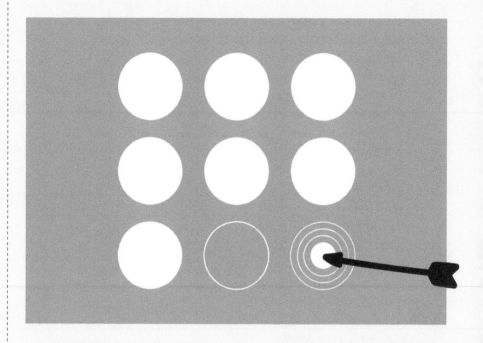

And finally... zoom in on your key points. Lead your listener to them with guile and preparation. You want them to reach the core of what you're saying. Take them to the point where they're hovering over and then zoom in. You can do that by pausing, taking a deep breath, and then vocally landing the big message. Then, pause again, look around and continue. I call this 'dropping the big one'. I recently heard an American presenter use a whisper to create atmosphere and suspense before she got her audience zooming in to the key point of her talk. It worked a treat.

A word about virtual communications. Nothing will beat the real experience of being in the room with your audience and throwing your eyes around the room and sensing, almost feeling and tasting, the energy. In the meantime, Zoom and other such tools have allowed for a new efficacy in our need to communicate, for which many people are truly grateful.

However, technology can itself be democratising: even politicians and expert communicators can be cut off by signal failures. Many of us have witnessed this when we've switched on our communication devices and had to wait patiently for the expert's face to unfreeze or the correspondent's link to reboot.

Do bear in mind that, once technology has taken hold, our voices are thinner and weaker, so we need to raise them. Remember to speak slowly, making your voice louder and clearer. There is a delay in delivery, so give your audience every opportunity to hear and understand. Hand movements also need to be slower and more purposeful; otherwise, your hands can look like strange, disembodied props flapping around and distracting the viewer.

However, this is your chance to really make the best of your background. Do make sure you have depth of vision behind you when you are showing off tasteful art and shelves of literature. If these features are too close, your audience will be more interested in spotting your reading material than the profundity of what you have to tell everyone. You need to send a subliminal message about your professionalism rather than distract from your message.

Hints and tips

Zoom is now a by-word for virtual communication, and so many people who are new to Zoom or Microsoft Teams have been caught out on the background. Check it out. If you are videoing from your home, please check that you are far enough away from the books so your listeners can't read the titles and move family photos away and extraneous clutter out of sight. Keep your background neutral so people will concentrate on what you're saying.

ABOUT THE AUTHOR

Wendy Smith is a writer, trainer and coach specialising in effective communication skills, from presenting and pitching to networking and assertiveness. Having enjoyed a career as a business writer for trade publications and national newspapers, Wendy branched out into training in 2000 after a suggestion from one of her colleagues that she might be cut out for it. Wendy obtained teaching qualifications and a master's degree in communications, and she trained as a coach to hone her knowledge. She set up her own company, Coralstone Training, and now works with designers and senior business people, teachers and students to help improve their overall performance and skills in communication.

www.coralstonetraining.com

Further Reading

Bird, Tom and Cassell, Jeremy *The Leaders Guide to Presenting* (Pearson Books, UK, 2017)

Crystal, David *The Gift of the Gab* (Yale University Press, UK, 2016)

Van Emden, Joan and Becker, Lucinda *Presentation Skills for Students* (Palgrave, UK, 2004 and 2010)

Runion, Meryl *How to Use Power Phrases* (McGraw-Hill, USA, 2004)

Gallo, Carmine *Talk Like Ted* (Macmillan, USA, 2014)

WORKING NOTES

WORKING NOTES

WORKING NOTES

Lightning Source UK Ltd.
Milton Keynes UK
UKHW021147030321
379663UK00007B/215